I Gave You My Heart

David Muncaster

SILVERMO☾N
PUBLISHING

www.silvermonpublishing.co.uk

© 2014 David Muncaster

SILVERMOON
P U B L I S H I N G

A Division of Silvermoon Productions Limited
3rd Floor I 207 Regent Street I London I W1B 3HH
0207 0961603
www.silvermoonpublishing.co.uk

ISBN 978-1-910457-01-6

Silvermoon Publishing is an innovative publishing house established to publish plays and license rights to theatre companies world-wide. Silvermoon aims to promote its plays and playwrights to ensure that its playwrights get maximum exposure.

In Theatres of Halls seating Four Hundred or more the fee will be subject to negotiation.

In Territories Overseas the fee quoted may not apply. A fee will be quoted on application to Silvermoon Publishing, London.

VIDEO-RECORDING OF AMATEUR PRODUCTIONS

Please note that the copyright laws governing video-recording are extremely complex and that it should not be assumed that any play may be video-recorded for whatever purpose without first obtaining the permission of the appropriate agents. The fact that a play is published by Silvermoon Publishing does not indicate that video rights are available or that Silvermoon Publishing control such rights.

PERFORMING LICENCE APPLICATIONS

A performing licence for these plays will be issued by "Silvermoon Publishing" subject to the following conditions:-

1. That the performance fee is paid in full on the date of application for a licence.
2. That the name of the author(s) is/are clearly shown in any programme or publicity material.
3. That the author(s) is/are entitled to receive two complimentary tickets to see his/her/their work in performance if they so wish.
4. That a copy of the play is purchased from Silvermoon Publishing for each named speaking part and a minimum of three copies purchased for backstage use.
5. That a copy of any reviews / Marketing materials be forwarded to Silvermoon Publishing.
6. That the Silvermoon Publishing licensing statement be displayed on any marketing material.

FEES

Details of script prices and fees payable for each performance or public reading can be obtained by telephone to (+44) 0207 0961603 or to the address below. Alternatively, latest prices can be obtained from our website. www.silvermoonpublishing.co.uk.

To apply for a performing licence for any play please write to Silvermoon Publishing, 3rd Floor, 207 Regent Street, London W1B 3HH or email via our website with the following details:-

1.   Name and address of theatre company.
2.   Details of venue including seating capacity.
3.   Dates of proposed performance or public reading.
4.   Contact telephone number for Author's complimentary tickets.

Or apply directly via our website at www.silvermoonpublishing.co.uk

PROFESSIONAL RIGHTS

Professional rights for Nativity should be addressed to Silvermoon Publishing.

DAVID MUNCASTER

Theatre has been part of David's life ever since his school days. He is on record for saying that drama studies were just about the only thing he was any good at, but turned down an opportunity to work at the Nottingham Playhouse as an Assistant Stage Manager because the cost of rent, food and bus fare were greater than the salary on offer. Instead he immersed himself into amateur theatre where he has done everything with the exception of prompt; which he wouldn't do "for all the tea in China"!

He began writing as a teenager, firstly lyrics for a rock band then articles for a student magazine before starting work on his first book. It took a surprising long time before David finally combined his passion for theatre with writing but his first play, *Call Girls* was an immediate success being published by New Theatre Publications and having performances in both the UK and the USA. Since then there have been hundreds of performances of David's work around the world by both amateur and professional companies with his festival friendly one act plays regularly winning awards.

In 2010 he answered an advertisement in Amateur Stage for a playscript reviewer and with an average of eight plays a month his reviews have become one of the most popular features in the magazine.

David lives in Cheshire where he is an active participant for two amateur groups and an enthusiastic supporter of all forms of theatre.

www.davidmuncaster.com

CHARACTERS

Kate, teens
Jenny, Kate's sister. A little younger.

I Gave You My Heart was first performed at Chelford Drama Festival June 2014 with the following cast:-

Kate: Alannah Roberts
Jenny: Rowan Perry

Directed by David Muncaster
Sound by Esme Perry

where it won the Adjudicator's Special Award presented by Greater Manchester Drama Federation. Adjudicator David Wood.

Lights up on KATE sitting on a couch in her living room. Next to her is a parcel which is square and about the size of a football. KATE is using a mobile device such as a smart phone or iPad. After a moment JENNY enters.

JENNY: That for me?

KATE: Is your name Kate?

JENNY: (*Sitting on the couch so that the parcel is between them.*) Ah. So, you gonna open it then?

KATE: Not sure.

JENNY: Kate! Stop texting will you? I'm talking to you.

KATE: You seem to have forgotten that I am not talking to you.

JENNY: Really? Sounds to me like you are talking to me. There's no one else around.

KATE: You know what I mean. I'm still angry with you.

JENNY: Oh come on Kate. It's been a week now.

KATE: A week in which you have apologised, let me see, how many times?

JENNY: OK, OK. I'm sorry.

KATE: Hm.

JENNY: I think the words you are looking for are "apology accepted".

KATE: A bit more sincerity might help.

JENNY: Look. I opened something addressed to you. It was a mistake.

KATE: It wasn't a mistake. You knew it was mine, you're just nosy. Shame for you that I caught you trying to reseal the envelope. How many letters of mine have you opened?

JENNY: I haven't done it before, honest.

KATE: I don't believe you.

JENNY: It's true. I don't know what made me do it. I was just bored.

KATE: I would never open anything of yours.

JENNY: OK. I'm sorry. Really, Sis.

KATE: That's better, (*Mimicking JENNY.*) "apology accepted".

(*goes back to using her smart phone.*)

JENNY: Who are you texting anyway?

KATE: I'm not texting, I'm on Dan's Facebook page.

JENNY: I thought you said you'd dumped him.

KATE: I have. I thought I'd heard the last of him until that turned up (*Indicating the parcel.*); it has his return address on it.

JENNY: Ahh. He has sent you a sweet little parting gift. How romantic.

KATE: Dan is not romantic, he's a weirdo; a freak. It's all your fault, Jenny; you set us up in the first place.

JENNY: Me?

KATE: You know you did.

JENNY: Oh, come on. You fancied him, don't deny it.

KATE: I did not.

JENNY: Oh come on, you couldn't take your eyes off him at that party.

KATE: You seem to have a rather different recollection of the events of that evening to me.

JENNY: You asked me to stop that nerd, Simon, from bothering you.

KATE: Yes.

JENNY:	So that you could make your move on Dan.
KATE:	No, not so that I could make a move on Dan; just so that Simon would stop making moves on me!
JENNY:	What's wrong with Simon, anyway? He's quite sweet.
KATE:	(*Putting on a nerd voice.*) "Did you know that there are up to four hundred billion stars in the galaxy, each of which could have any number of planets. It is almost certain that somewhere out there another Simon is talking to another Kate at another party."
JENNY:	Well, that's interesting. Isn't it?
KATE:	(*Still with a nerd voice.*) "Which means that someone out there is as lucky as me"
JENNY:	How lovely! You get educated and chatted up at the same time!

KATE imitates throwing up.

JENNY:	Anyway, I don't see the problem. You're a bit of a nerd yourself.
KATE:	How dare you! I'm a geek. There is a subtle difference.
JENNY:	So I dive in and rescue you. Risk being nerded to death myself for the sake of my big sister and what thanks do I get?
KATE:	Oh yeah. Thanks.
JENNY:	I was doing you a favour, it's not my fault Dan didn't come up to your exacting standards. What's wrong with him, anyway? He didn't seem weird.
KATE:	You are kidding! You really don't know what he's like, do you? He is so possessive. Whenever I added a friend on Facebook he'd be asking, "Who it is?" "How do you know them?" Do you remember that time I lost my phone? He had it. He was texting my contacts pretending to be me.

JENNY: Well, yeah. Sounds a bit extreme, I suppose. How do you mean pretending to be you?

KATE: Just that. Fraping me.

JENNY: I thought you could only get fraped on Facebook.

KATE: Well, whatever. That's what he was doing anyway.

JENNY: Anyway, you can talk. The amount of times you've fraped me.

KATE: That's different. Everyone knows it's just me messing about. Unless your friends genuinely believe that you are going to go on Facebook and update your status to say that you've spent the whole morning in the toilet trying to flush away a massive poo.

JENNY: I still haven't forgiven you for that.

KATE: Dan was really pretending to be me. Hoping that someone would incriminate me.

JENNY: Incriminate you! How?

KATE: For example he sent Paul a text saying, "I really love it when we get together - kiss, kiss, kiss".

JENNY: To Paul!

KATE: Because he saw a text from Paul that said "You did well last night." Or something like that.

JENNY: I take it that he doesn't know that Paul is your music tutor and that he is about ninety.

KATE: He's so jealous. I tell you, he's a freak. When I eventually got my phone back he made out that he'd only just found it and that it had wiped itself. All my text messages had gone. It was only when I next saw Paul that I realised that he was lying.

JENNY: Awkward.

KATE: You're telling me. I went to his house for my lesson and

	Paul's wife was sat there which I thought was a bit odd, but then he started going on about how he had a bit of a crush on his music teacher when he was a boy, and I'm thinking, "I don't want to know this" but then he started saying that it's "natural" and that I'd "grow out of it" and I went, "Hang on. What are you talking about?"
JENNY:	Très Awkward.
KATE:	So when he explained about the text message I don't know who was more embarrassed: me or him.
JENNY:	I'm amazed you've ever gone back there.
KATE:	We've never spoken about it again. But then I started asking around my mates and they said that they'd had weird text messages as well and that's when I knew that I had to finish with him.
JENNY:	I never got a weird message off him.
KATE:	He'd hardly likely to send one to you is he?
JENNY:	So let me guess. He didn't take it well?
KATE:	He went ballistic! Saying he was going to kill himself, and you know what, Jenny? I wouldn't put it past him. Really. I wouldn't put anything past him. He was texting me every five minutes, writing on my wall, messaging me and then, two days ago, it stopped.
JENNY:	So? Result! That's what you want isn't it?
KATE:	This is serious, Jenny. I told you, he's a maniac. Capable of anything. Do you know the last thing he said? It was a message on my Facebook wall. "I gave you my heart."

After a pause of a few moments they both turn to look at the parcel.

JENNY:	Oh, that's ridiculous. How's he gonna write on Facebook after he's hacked out one of his vital organs?
KATE:	He could have written it first.
JENNY:	Then he cut out his heart, put it in a box, sealed it and

	addressed it to you; not forgetting to add his return address in case you were away.
KATE:	He could have had an accomplice.
JENNY:	And I could have a sister with an over active imagination. Oh, come on Kate, let's just open it.
KATE:	No!
JENNY:	OK. Throw it away then.
KATE:	No!
JENNY:	Make you mind up. All right, I'm going to open it.
KATE:	Don't Jenny!
JENNY:	So what are you going to do? Just sit here and stare at it?
KATE:	I don't know what to do.
JENNY:	Look. It isn't going to be any part of his anatomy, is it?
KATE:	I don't know.
JENNY:	Realistically.
KATE:	I suppose.
JENNY:	So, if it is something nasty, whatever it is, I will just throw it away. OK? You don't even have to look at it.
KATE:	Are you sure?
JENNY:	Oh, let's just do it.

JENNY rips open the box, looks inside and screams.

KATE:	What is it?
JENNY:	(*Pulling a smaller box from the outside one and grinning.*) Another box. Whatever it is, it is well packed.
KATE:	You idiot. You scared me. Just get on with it.

JENNY:	I thought you didn't want to open it.
KATE:	You've started now.
JENNY:	Do you know, I don't think I'll bother.
KATE:	Just get on with it!
JENNY:	OK, OK.

JENNY opens the box to find – another box.

JENNY:	What is this? Russian dolls?
KATE:	It's just Dan playing his mind games. I give up. Just throw it away. I don't want to know.
JENNY:	OK.
KATE:	Wait!
JENNY:	Make your mind up will you?
KATE:	Why? Why do I have to make my mind up? I was sat here, minding my own business, happily not making my mind up until you walked in. Why do I have to do what you tell me?
JENNY:	Because I'm always right?
KATE:	I'm not kidding. I've had it with you now.
JENNY:	OK, OK. Calm down! I didn't know you were so uptight.
KATE:	I am not uptight.
JENNY:	OK. You want to be on your own. I'm going. I'm gone.
KATE:	Good.
JENNY:	I'm not here.
KATE:	Right.
JENNY:	I'm elsewhere.

KATE: OK! Shut up! Stay if you want but keep your mouth shut.

JENNY: (*Through a closed mouth.*) Mmm, mmm, mmm.

KATE: You're such an idiot.

JENNY: Mank myoo

KATE: Jenny.

JENNY: Mmm?

KATE: Can you do something for me?

JENNY: Mot?

KATE: OK, you can stop keeping your mouth shut now.

JENNY: You're so kind.

KATE: Would you do me a favour?

JENNY: A favour? Of course, sweet pea. Anything for you.

KATE: Would you call him for me?

JENNY: Call Dan?

KATE: No, the Pope. Of course, Dan. Who else are we talking about?

JENNY: Well, seeing as you are being so sweet about it. What do you want me to say to him?

KATE: Nothing.

JENNY: You just want me to hang up as soon as he answers. Is that it?

KATE: Yes. No. I don't know.

JENNY: Why don't you ring him? You can hang up just as well as me.

KATE: He'll recognise my number.

JENNY:	I see. If he's the freak you say he is I'm not sure I really want him to have my number in his contacts.
KATE:	You could put in that number in front - so that the person you are calling doesn't see your number.
JENNY:	You could put in that number in front so that the person you are calling doesn't see your number.
KATE:	Oh please, Jenny.
JENNY:	Go on then. Give me his number. Anything for a quite life.

KATE finds the number on her phone and shows it to JENNY who dials.

KATE:	Make sure he speaks so you know that it's him.
JENNY:	I thought you wanted me to hang up.
KATE:	Just make sure it is him.
JENNY:	Make your... Hello? Oh, Hi Dan, it's Jenny...
KATE:	Hang up!
JENNY:	Kate's sister. What do you mean which one? How many Kates do you know? Oh, I see what you mean. Her younger sister. The good looking one.
KATE:	Give me the phone.
JENNY:	I'll tell you why I'm calling. I just wondered if you fancied popping round because...
KATE:	I said, give me the phone. (*She grabs it, puts it to her ear, then to JENNY:*) Very funny.
JENNY:	You must have given me the wrong number.
KATE:	Don't be stupid. You must have misdialled.
JENNY:	OK. (*Sighs.*) Show me your phone. I'll try again.
KATE:	Oh don't bother. What's the point?

JENNY: I don't know what the point is. I was doing what you wanted me to. I rather thought you knew what the point was, as it was you that issued me with the instructions.

KATE: You can be so pompous sometimes.

JENNY: I refer you to my previous statement regarding the aforementioned accusation.

KATE: Very funny.

JENNY: Thank you. I was rather pleased with it myself.

KATE: Look, Jenny, why don't you just go to hell.

JENNY: OK. See you there.

KATE: And take that bloody box with you.

JENNY: I'm opening it.

KATE: No!

JENNY: Come on, Kate. How bad can it be?

KATE: Very bad. That's how bad it could be. Unbelievably, scarily, totally bad. The guy's out of his mind.

JENNY: Be that as it may, but I'm pretty sure that he hasn't sent you one of his organs. Unless it's his...

KATE: I wouldn't even put that past him.

JENNY: It might explain the ever decreasing box size.

KATE: Don't even joke about it.

JENNY: It's not very likely though is it? Really?

KATE: Yeah, but think about what he said. "I gave you my heart". Whatever is in that box is related to that sentence.

JENNY: I think we are entering the realms of fantasy here. Or horror.

KATE:	Why?
JENNY:	I think we've agreed that it can't be his heart: so what? He's just slaughtered some random stranger?
KATE:	It could be a pig's heart. Or something gross like that.
JENNY:	Eww.
KATE:	Exactly.
JENNY:	I hadn't thought of that.
KATE:	Clearly.
JENNY:	Would he do that?
KATE:	Have you been listening to anything I've told you?
JENNY:	So we just throw it away. No question. I don't know why you are even thinking about opening it. It's not going to be anything nice: let's just throw it away and forget about it.
KATE:	But we have a responsibility don't we?
JENNY:	A what?
KATE:	I mean. If he has done something (*Pause.*) bad, I mean really bad, we have to do something. Go to the police or something.
JENNY:	We?
KATE:	OK, me then.
JENNY:	Kate. Listen to me. The guy is a freak; you've convinced me of that, and maybe there is some hideous bit of an animal in there, or maybe it is something else equally unpleasant but, whatever it is, it is not your responsibility. I seriously doubt that it could be anything that we would need to report to the police. He's a freak and he wants to hurt you but he's not going to do anything that would get him into trouble. The sensible thing is for me to just take it out and put it in the bin and for you to forget all about Dan and get on with your life.

19

KATE: I don't know.

JENNY: We'll be laughing about this in six months.

KATE: OK. OK, yes. Take it. Take it out and throw it away.

JENNY: Are you sure?

KATE: Yes. You're right. I'm not going to let him play mind games any more.

JENNY: You've made the right decision.

JENNY picks up the box and, as she exits, the sisters look at each other and smile. There is a sense of support: the love that squabbling siblings occasionally show each other. After JENNY exits KATE becomes uncomfortable. She is listening intently trying to hear what her sister is doing. Eventually she calls out to her.

KATE: What are you doing Jenny?

JENNY: (*Off.*) Just gathering up the rubbish.

KATE: You're not opening it are you?

JENNY: (*Off.*) I told you I'm just...

JENNY suddenly lets out a high-pitched scream. She has obviously opened then box and whatever was inside has given her a huge shock. KATE smiles a knowing smile.

KATE: (*Quietly*) Oh Jenny. You are so predictable. (*She picks up her mobile device and makes a call.*) It's me. Mission accomplished, she completely fell for it, believed everything I said about you. Of course she opened it, I told you she would. But what did you put in there, Dan, she's totally freaked out? (*As KATE waits for an answer JENNY re-enters unseen by her carrying a very small box.*) What do you mean, I'll soon find out? We agreed that you were going to put a heart shaped cushion in there. The fun starts when you turn up here. What was it, Dan? What did you put in there? I hope it wasn't something really gross; it was just a joke, you know. I didn't want to scare her, just get my own back.

JENNY comes into KATE's line of sight, opens the box and takes out a ring.

JENNY: I guess he has given you his heart. (*She takes KATE's left hand and slips the ring onto her finger.*) Congratulations.

KATE looks at the ring, at the mobile device, at JENNY. She is, for once, speechless. JENNY smiles.

END

OTHER PLAYS BY DAVID MUNCASTER

Silvermoon Publishing
www.silvermoonpublishing.co.uk

The World and its Arse
Everyone's A Twinner
The Beginners Guide To Murdering Your Husband

New Theatre Publications
www.plays4theatre.com

Call Girls
Community Spirit
Fresh Flowers for the Thirsting Flowers
Mad Gary's Fruit and Nut Case
Mission Impossible
Waiting for a Train

YouthPlays
www.youthplays.com

The Kennel Club

Jasper Publications
www.jasperpubllishing.com

Life Begins at Seventy
Life Begins Again

OTHER PUBLICATIONS

Silvermoon Publishing

The Play's The Thing 1 - Collected Play Reviews
The Play's The Thing 2- Collected Play Reviews

OTHER PLAYS PUBLISHED BY
SILVERMOON PUBLISHING

The Beginner's Guide To Murdering Your Husband
or (Ten Easy Steps To Becoming A Widow)
Unwisely written by David Muncaster
(3f,2m)
This play is presented as though it is an instructional video that the audience are watching being filmed. Maddy will present a variety of methods for disposing of an unwanted husband, aided by Jim, her real life husband, and her faithful employees. But is she really trying to get rid of her husband? Is the video just a ruse to lull him into a false sense of security? The parallels with their real life relationship give Jim plenty to worry about but, as the play reaches its its climax, we realise that nothing is what it seems. Criss-cross indeed!

The World and its Arse
by David Muncaster
(6m,6f)
Frank's mind plays tricks on him as horrors from his past torment him. Len has nothing but memories. Brian doesn't know what he's got. He probably shouldn't even be there but he has nowhere else to go. A few days in an NHS ward give us a glimpse into the lives of a diverse set of people.

You see all sorts in here
Any colour, any class, any religion
Disease doesn't discriminate
You get the world and its arse come through that door

Nativity
by Jonathan Hall
(2m, 3f)
It's December 1979 and class 2G are getting ready for the school Nativity. Gemma wants to be Mary but because she's got a big loud voice she's the narrator, and anyway Sarah her best friend is far loads prettier than her, everyone says so. And as for Kirsty- she doesn't even get a look in, not that she cares, she's bothered about showing her knickers in the practical area. And of course there can only be one choice for Joseph, and that'd have to be Tony, everyone's favourite, complete with his thirteen colour biro. And Nicholas? In love with Sarah and dreams of flying through the milky way with her in the TARDIS? He's always going to be the Innkeeper.

Nativity is about the play we've all been in. About tea towels on heads and coconut-shell donkey hooves. Dinner ladies and toilet roll angels, reading books and Blue Peter. It's about our six year old selves, the adults that shaped us, the dreams that lit our days- and the people we have become.

Flushed
by Ron Nicol
(3f) One Act
It's a singles night, and Jan and Meg are taking a break in the Ladies Room. Jan is criticising Tara, unaware that Tara is hiding in one of the toilet cubicles. When Tara's presence is revealed a fight ensues and Jan confesses the reason for her jealousy. Then Meg discovers that the door to the room seems to be locked, and the succeeding series of mishaps and misfortunes ruins Jan's appearance and assurance. Tara eventually manages to open the door, but on the threshold of escape they find that Meg is trapped in one of the cubicles.

The only monthly magazine passionate about amateur theatre